STARS AND PLANETS

STARS AND PLANETS

BY ALICE FIELDS

Illustrated by Michael Tregenza

An Easy-Read Fact Book
FRANKLIN WATTS
New York/London/Toronto/Sydney/1980

Thanks are due to the following for
kind permission to reproduce photographs:
Edinburgh Observatory; Hale Observatories;
Mansell Picture Library; National Aeronautics
and Space Administration (NASA);
Ann Ronan Picture Library;
Royal Greenwich Observatory;
United States Travel Service;
Woodmansterne NASA.

The Publishers would like to thank Dr. John Guest and
Dr. D. C. B. Whittet for their help with this project.

Library of Congress Cataloging in Publication Data

Fields, Alice.
    Stars and planets.

    (An Easy-read fact book)
    Includes index.
    SUMMARY: Describes the sun, the planets
which orbit it, and other phenomena of the universe,
including asteroids, comets, meteors, and other
stars and galaxies.
    1. Astronomy—Juvenile literature. [1.
Astronomy] I. Tregenza, Michael. II. Title.
QB46.F53   523   79-25452
        ISBN 0-531-03247-7

R.L. 3.3 Spache Revised Formula

Voyager spacecraft

We live in the **Space Age**. It is a time when many scientific adventures are possible.

Astronauts have walked on the **Moon**. It is no longer just a mysterious shining shape in the night sky. Trips to the Moon have helped scientists gather useful information. **Unmanned spacecraft** send pictures of other **planets** back to **Earth**.

An age of discovery is just beginning. There is still much to learn about what we see in the sky.

On a clear night, the sky may be full of **stars**. Sometimes you can count hundreds of them.

You may also see one or two planets. Planets revolve (circle) around stars.

Stars and planets both look like small points of twinkling lights in the sky. But these lights do not really twinkle. The air is always moving and that is why they seem to twinkle.

The light and dark sides of Earth, seen from the Sun

We think of stars as being visible only at night. However, the **Sun** is also a star.

Like all stars, the Sun produces its own **light** and **heat**. Planets cannot do this. They are able to shine at night because they **reflect** (bounce back) light from the Sun. Planets are somewhat like enormous mirrors.

Our home, Earth, is a planet. It is like a giant ball spinning in space.

As Earth **rotates** (turns), it is daylight on the part facing the Sun. It is night on the side away from the Sun.

The other planets also rotate. They rotate at different speeds. Some move more quickly than Earth and others more slowly.

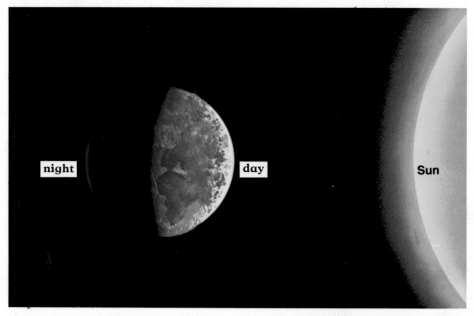

Earth reflecting light from the Sun

At the present time, there are **nine** known planets. Someday, more may be discovered in the **Universe** (that vast and unlimited area of space).

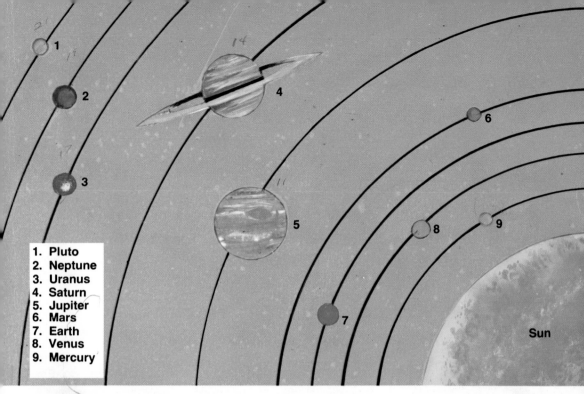

1. Pluto
2. Neptune
3. Uranus
4. Saturn
5. Jupiter
6. Mars
7. Earth
8. Venus
9. Mercury

Sun

The orbits of the planets around the Sun. Orbit of Pluto shown as it will be after 1999. Pluto is presently closer to the Sun than Neptune.

These nine planets move around our Sun in the same direction. Each moves in its own oval path, called an **orbit**.

The one nearest to the Sun is **Mercury**. Then comes **Venus, Earth, Mars, Jupiter, Saturn, Uranus, Neptune,** and **Pluto**.

Those closer to the Sun have smaller orbits. They need less time to complete one **revolution** (go around the Sun once).

It takes Earth 365 days (one year) to complete one orbit, or revolution. Mercury, the nearest planet to the Sun, takes only 88 days. Far-off Pluto needs nearly 248 *years* to complete one orbit.

The Sun, together with all the planets, and other bodies that revolve around it, make up what is known as the **Solar System**.

Each month the Moon seems to go through stages. It starts out as a round ball (full), eventually becomes a thin sliver, and ends up full again. This is because the amount of light the Moon reflects to Earth varies as the positions of the Moon, Sun, and Earth change.

A view of the Moon, as it looked from the *Apollo* spacecraft

The Moon, a member of the Solar System, is a **satellite** (a small object orbiting a planet) of Earth. It revolves around Earth once a month.

At night we see light and dark patches on the Moon's surface. The light parts are mountain regions. The dark areas are valleys or plains. The Moon is also full of very large **craters** (holes).

Early **astronomers** (scientists who study objects in the sky) thought the dark areas were **lunar** (moon) **seas**. But since men have traveled to the Moon, we know that this is not true.

We now know that the Moon is a place without water or air.

Mercury is one of the smallest planets in our Solar System. It is 1,000 miles (1,609 km) larger than the Moon, and it also has a surface full of craters.

The daylight side of Mercury is very close to the Sun. It is so hot on that side that no form of life could exist there. On the other side of the planet, away from the Sun, everything is **frozen**.

Mercury

Venus

Venus shines brighter than any other star or planet in the night sky. It looks that bright to us because it is the nearest planet to Earth.

Venus is covered with thick layers of **clouds**. The clouds reflect some of the light coming from the Sun. These clouds also hide the surface of Venus from astronomers who look at the sky through **telescopes**.

Unmanned spacecraft have been able to give us some information about Venus. We now know that it is a place where human beings could not live.

The air is thick with poisonous gases. Clouds of **sulfuric acid** are so heavy that their weight would crush a person.

The surface of Venus

Carbon dioxide in the atmosphere holds in heat. This makes the surface very hot. An astronaut would quickly burn up on Venus.

A storm on Venus might look like this.

Venus appears to be a hazy red color during the day. This is because dense clouds keep sunlight from reaching the surface directly. At night there are **lightning storms** on Venus.

Venus is almost as large as Earth. But, very little is known about this mysterious planet.

Mars is a bright red and often called the **Red Planet**. Together with its two satellites (moons) **Phobos** and **Deimos**, Mars has always had a very special attraction for us.

Many people believed that there was **life** on Mars. Some used to think they could see **irrigation canals** (ditches that bring water to dry land) on its surface, built by **Martians** (people from Mars).

Astronomers now know that most of the surface of Mars is a rocky desert, and that there are no irrigation canals.

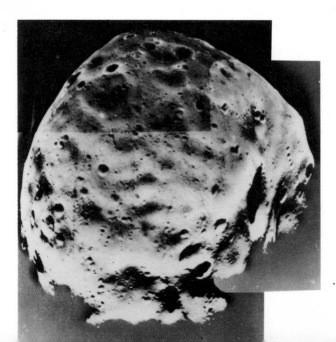

Phobos, a satellite of Mars

At opposite ends of Mars there are great white patches of ice. These are called **Polar Caps**.

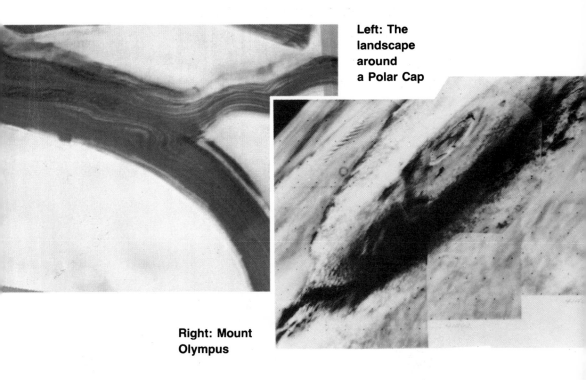

Left: The
landscape
around
a Polar Cap

Right: Mount
Olympus

Near the **equator** (center) of Mars, there are huge **volcanoes**. One of these volcanoes has been named **Olympus Mons** (Mount Olympus). It is 15½ miles (25 km) high—more than twice the size of the largest volcano on Earth.

General conditions on Mars have been studied. It is now known that the forms of life that exist on Earth do not live on Mars. But, could simple **organisms** (living things) exist in the soil of Mars?

Two unmanned **Viking spacecraft** landed on Mars in 1976. Various tests were carried out on the soil. But no living things were found.

Only when astronauts are able to explore Mars, will we know whether any form of life exists there.

The rocky surface of Mars. Large amounts of iron in the soil make it a reddish color.

The giant planet Uranus

Beyond Mars are Jupiter, Saturn, Uranus, and Neptune, the four giants of the Solar System.

These bodies are not like the other rocky planets. Instead, they are mainly gases—**hydrogen, helium, ammonia**, and **methane**. As these gases cool, they turn into liquids. Further cooling causes them to freeze.

Because of these conditions, there is little chance that there is life on these four planets.

Jupiter is the largest known planet. It is more than 1,300 times bigger than Earth and has fourteen, possibly fifteen satellites (moons).

Jupiter is about 400 million miles (600 million km) from Earth. But it is large, and its clouds reflect a lot of sunlight. It can be seen without a telescope.

Jupiter, as it might look seen from its satellite, Europa.
Right: Jupiter and its four largest satellites.

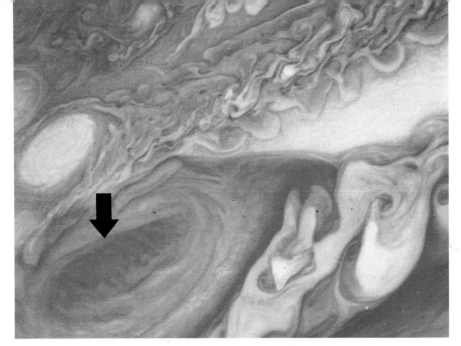

The surface of Jupiter, showing the Great Red Spot

Jupiter has a huge mark known as the **Great Red Spot**. It measures about 25,000 miles (40,000 km) by 8,000 miles (13,000 km).

The mark is thought to be a swirling mass of gases, or a constant storm. It moves slowly across the planet.

Sometimes the Great Red Spot is not so bright. And sometimes, it even disappears for a while.

Io is the most famous of Jupiter's thirteen satellites. It is about the size of our Moon.

Voyager I has taken some pictures of Io. They show large and active volcanoes. These volcanoes **erupt** (explode) at speeds of up to 932 miles (1,500 km) per hour.

Io is one of the strangest satellites in the Solar System.

Io

Saturn is twice as far from the Sun as Jupiter. Saturn has a set of **rings** around it. These rings are really dust, ice, and rock fragments.

Saturn

It was always thought that Saturn has ten satellites. But in September 1979, an eleventh satellite was discovered, as well as another ring.

The **Pioneer Spacecraft** helped to make these discoveries.

In spite of its size, Saturn is a light planet when compared to others.

Much less is known about the other two giant planets—Uranus and Neptune. They are known as the twin planets and are about half the size of Saturn.

Uranus has five satellites and a set of rings. It is an unusual planet because it lies on its side.

The "poles" of Uranus lie on its side.

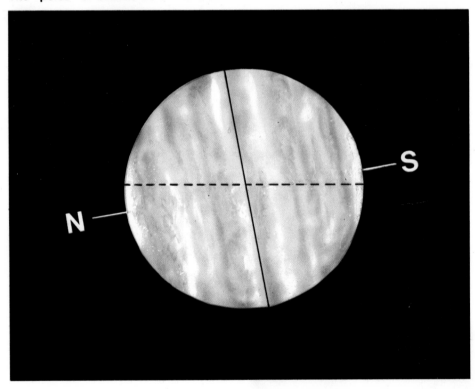

Pictured here, Neptune, the Roman god of the sea. Many of the planets are named after ancient Greek and Roman gods.

Neptune is a planet that seems to be blue. It has two satellites, **Triton** and **Nereid**. Some people have thought that Pluto may also have once been a satellite of Neptune.

Pluto, the smallest planet, is only about 1,500 miles (2,414 km) in diameter and has one satellite. On an average, Pluto is farther from the Sun than any other planet.

Pluto's orbit sometimes crosses over, or travels inside Neptune's orbit.

In the year 1989, Pluto will be at its closest to Earth. Unmanned spacecraft will be busy seeking more information about it.

Is Pluto really the most distant planet of our Solar System? Perhaps there is a tenth planet waiting to be discovered. After all, Pluto was not discovered until 1930!

The 1973 launching of *Mariner 10* to Venus and Mercury

Will asteroids be a source of minerals in the future?

Other bodies besides the planets orbit the Sun. The **Asteroid Belt** lies between Mars and Jupiter.

Asteroids are chunks of rock, orbiting the Sun in a circular path. They may be **debris** (remains) of other planets. Few asteroids are larger than 100 miles (160 km) in diameter.

In the future, Earth's mineral supply may become scarce. Then, asteroids might be a new source for mining needed minerals.

Comets sometimes visit the inner Solar System. They are masses of ice, gas, and dust.

Comets can be seen only when they are close to the Sun. As a comet passes the Sun, part of its gassy surface heats and forms a glowing tail.

Some comets have very long orbits that can take up to 75,000 years to complete. These are known as **long-term** comets.

Engraving of a comet seen above Paris in 1811

Comet

Those with smaller orbits are called **short-term** comets. An example is **Haley's comet**, which reappears every 76 years. It is due in 1986.

Astronomers estimate that there are about 100,000 million comets. Most of them are long-term comets.

Bright comets can sometimes be seen in broad daylight. Their tails may stretch almost half-way across the sky.

Sometimes pieces break off comets and enter Earth's atmosphere. Friction with the atmosphere causes them to burn. This produces glowing streaks in the sky called **meteors** or **shooting stars**.

Larger rocky **fragments** (pieces) occasionally journey through the atmosphere without burning up and crash into Earth. These rocks from outer space are called **meteorites**. When they hit the ground they form large craters. Fortunately, such meteorites are very rare.

A crater made by a meteorite in the Arizona desert

Gravity is a powerful force in space. It keeps the Moon in its path around Earth. Gravity keeps the planets circling through the Solar System. On Earth, gravity helps keep our feet on the ground. Without it, we might float off into space!

Dotted lines represent the force of gravity pulling everything toward the center of Earth.

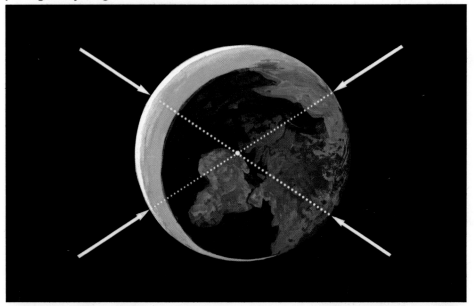

The Sun is very important to us as a source of **solar energy** (light and heat). Without the Sun, life on Earth would not be possible.

Solar energy is produced by an explosive **atomic reaction** that changes **hydrogen** to **helium** at a rate of 600 million tons per second. The surface temperature of the Sun is 6,000°C. But in the center, the heat from the constant explosions brings the temperature up to 15 million degrees Celsius.

Solar energy will continue for thousands of millions of years. We know this because of the Sun's size. It could easily swallow nearly 1.3 million planets the size of Earth.

The different layers of the Sun.

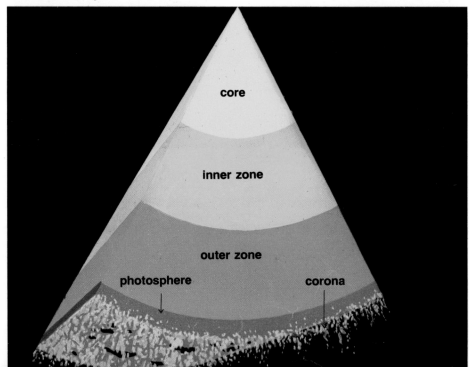

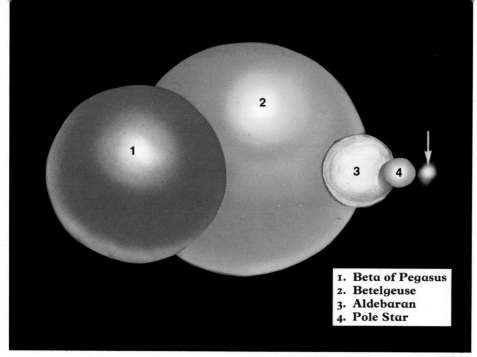

1. Beta of Pegasus
2. Betelgeuse
3. Aldebaran
4. Pole Star

Diagram shows the size of the Sun (arrow) compared to larger stars.

There are many stars even more powerful than the Sun.

The Sun seems larger and hotter than the other stars, because it is much closer to us. It is 93 million miles (150 million km) away from Earth.

The next nearest star, **Proxima Centauri**, is about 24 million million miles (39 million million km) away. Proxima Centauri is 270 thousand times further away from Earth than the Sun.

Scientists know that the surface of the Sun has many disturbances. Dark marks, called **sunspots**, sometimes appear on the Sun's surface. They are usually accompanied by violent bursts of **radiation** (explosions of particles of energy).

We see these bursts of radiation as very bright **solar flares**. They often interfere with radio communications on Earth. Scientists are still trying to discover the exact cause of sunspots.

Photograph of the Sun showing sunspots

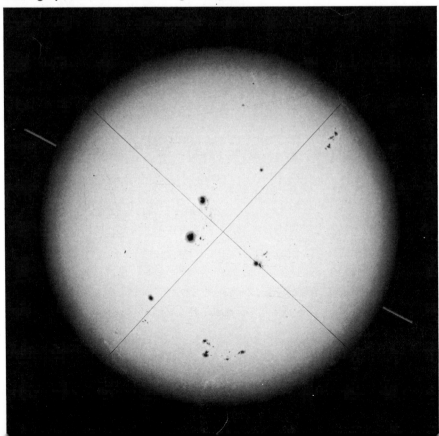

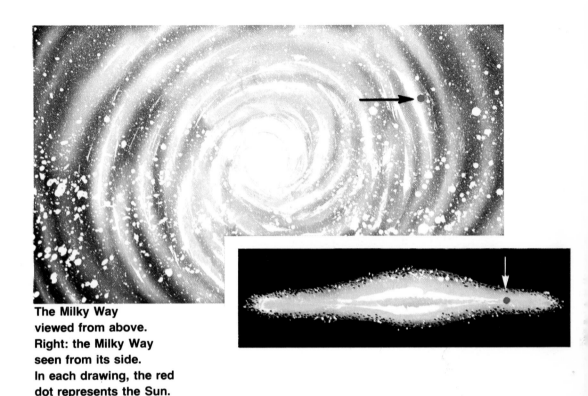

The Milky Way
viewed from above.
Right: the Milky Way
seen from its side.
In each drawing, the red
dot represents the Sun.

As the planets are moving in their orbits around the Sun, the Sun is also revolving. It is part of a vast turning spiral of stars called a **Galaxy**.

Our Galaxy is called the **Milky Way**. It contains about 100,000 million stars.

From outside our Galaxy, the Milky Way may look like an enormous pinwheel in the sky. But looking up from Earth, we see the Milky Way only as a fuzzy band across the sky.

There are many different stars in our Galaxy. Some are yellow, like the Sun.

Hotter stars, such as **Sirius**, appear to be blue and white. Cooler stars are much redder and sometimes very big.

Antares is a red supergiant. It is so big that, if it were to change places with the Sun, it would extend beyond Earth. And it would fill the orbit of Mars, too.

Some stars appear to be single points of light. But they are really two or more stars very close to each other.

When only two stars are involved, they are called a **binary system**. One of the pair is usually much brighter than the other. When one of the pair passes directly in front of the other, it becomes dimmer.

Binary stars seen through a
telescope. Often, the two stars
are of different coloring.

Alpha of Hercules

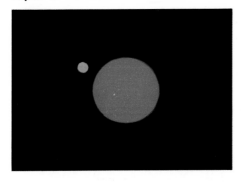

Alpha of the Scorpion

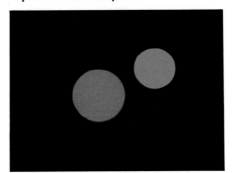

Beta of the Scorpion

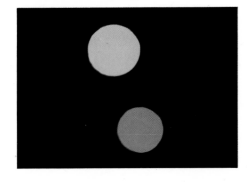

Beta of Orion

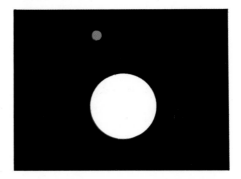

Gamma of Delphinius

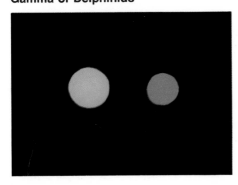

Epsilon of Boötes

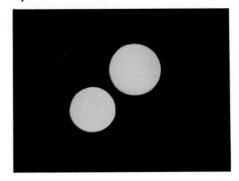

The bright star **Algol** has a companion star that passes in front of it every two days. Therefore, the brilliance of Algol changes frequently.

Other stars show changes in brightness as they shrink and swell (change in size). **Mira** is an example of this type of **variable** star.

Occasionally, an unknown star will burst into brilliance for a short time. Then it fades away again. This is caused by explosions in the outer layers of the star. It is called a **nova**.

It is very rare that a star may explode completely, becoming even brighter than a nova. Then it is called a **supernova**. One supernova was witnessed by the Chinese in the year 1054. The remains of this explosion are still visible in the sky. They are part of the **Crab Nebula**. A nebula is a cloud of dust and gas, from which stars are formed.

A supernova, such as the Crab Nebula (shown on page 40), might produce a gas cloud like the Orion Nebula (right), where new stars could form.

In 1968 a strange star, called a **pulsar** (sends out spurts of energy), was finally located inside the Crab Nebula.

A pulsar is extremely heavy. A matchbox-size piece of it would weigh over 10 million tons. The pulsar in the Crab Nebula seems to be a fragment of a larger star that exploded in 1054.

Crab Nebula

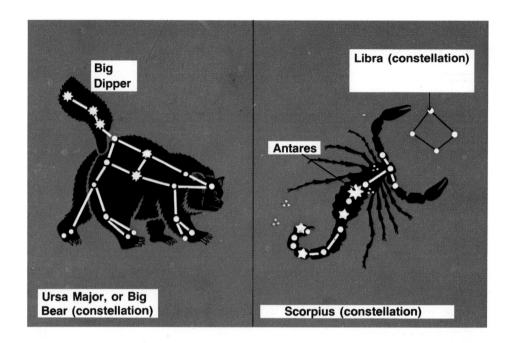

Big
Dipper

Libra (constellation)

Antares

Ursa Major, or Big
Bear (constellation)

Scorpius (constellation)

Stars are always moving rapidly through space. But they are so far away that they appear to keep to the same patterns.

Ancient astronomers named these patterns, or **constellations**, after gods, heroes, and animals. An example is **Ursa Major** (the **Great Bear**). It can be seen in the northern skies throughout the entire year.

Pleiades

The stars in a constellation are not usually grouped together. When seen from Earth, they appear to lie in the same direction.

However, you can also see groups of stars that really are huddled together in the sky.

These star clusters are groups of stars within our Galaxy. The **Pleiades**, or "**Seven Sisters**," are a well-known example of such a cluster. Larger groups may contain up to one million stars.

The space between the stars is filled by a very thinly-spread mass of gas and dust. This collects in places to form large clouds, or **nebulae.**

Lagoon Nebula

If a nebula contains some stars, it will look like a bright haze in the sky. The **Orion Nebula**, pictured on page 39, is an example.

If a nebula does not contain any stars, it remains dark. It blocks the light from those stars that lie behind it.

Dark nebulae were once thought to be holes in the sky. An example of this is the **Horsehead Nebula**, which is close to the Orion Nebula.

Horsehead Nebula

Optical telescope

Astronomers are constantly studying the universe with powerful telescopes. They have discovered a number of galaxies different from our own.

One of the nearest to us is the spiral **Andromeda** galaxy. Light travels faster than anything else we know of. Yet, it takes about two million years for light to reach us from the Andromeda galaxy. Therefore, we know that Andromeda is two million **light-years** away.

The most distant galaxies are over a thousand times farther away than Andromeda. Nobody knows what might lie beyond them.

Since 1961, when the Soviet Union launched their unmanned space probe, **Venera I**, scientists have learned a lot. Thirty-nine space probes later, they have learned more about how the solar system was created (made) than they had learned in the past 2,500 years.

But what of the future? A famous space scientist says, "Every successive major discovery proves that our universe is not in the center of everything."

There is still a great deal to learn to help us unlock the mysteries of the universe.